ERACY NEWS LITERACY NEW

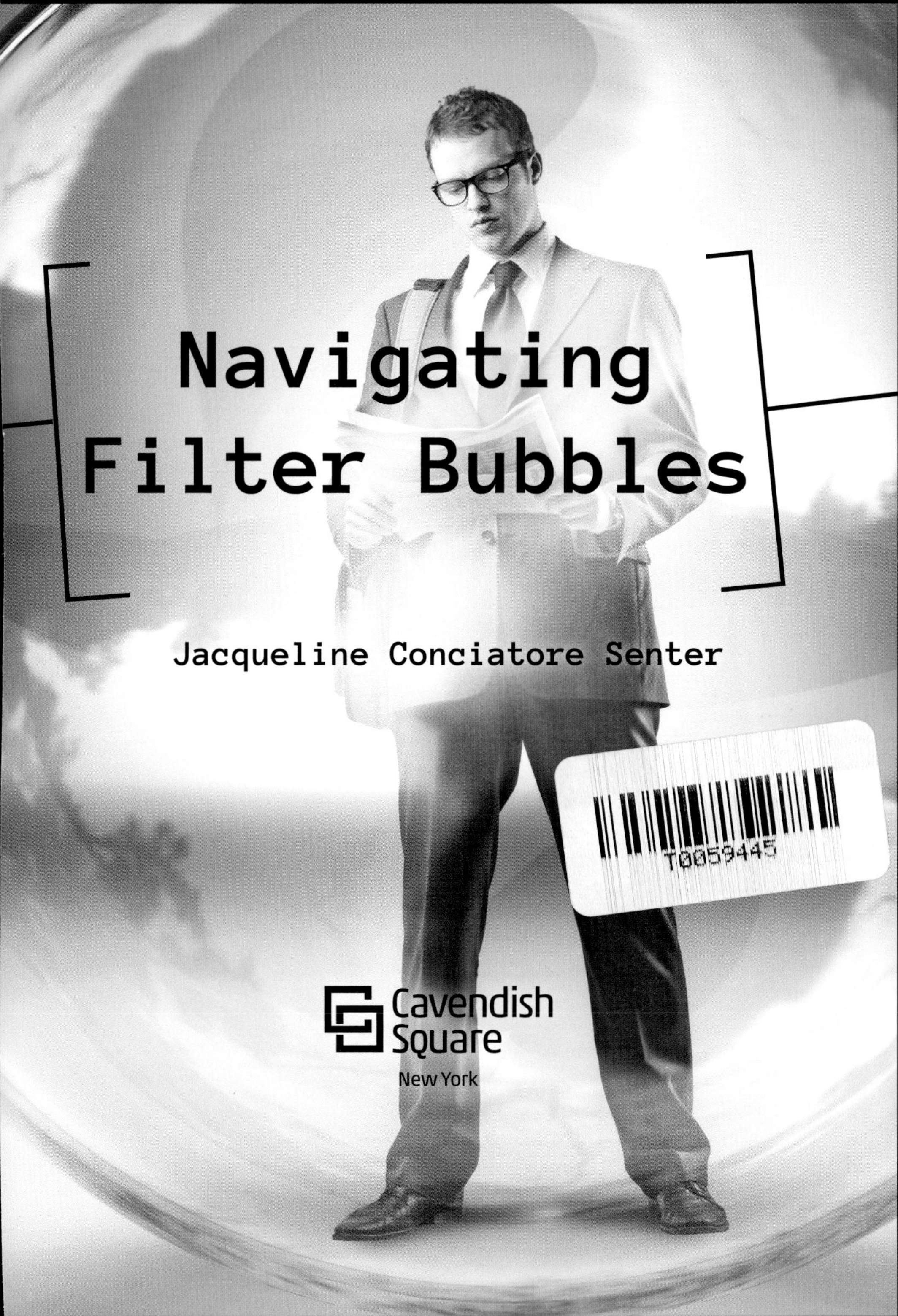

Navigating Filter Bubbles

Jacqueline Conciatore Senter

Cavendish Square
New York

Published in 2019 by Cavendish Square Publishing, LLC
243 5th Avenue, Suite 136, New York, NY 10016

Copyright © 2019 by Cavendish Square Publishing, LLC

First Edition

Website: cavendishsq.com

This publication represents the opinions and views of the author based on
his or her personal experience, knowledge, and research. The information
in this book serves as a general guide only. The author and publisher
have used their best efforts in preparing this book and disclaim liability
rising directly or indirectly from the use and application of this book.

All websites were available and accurate when this book was sent to press.

Library of Congress Cataloging-in-Publication Data

Names: Senter, Jacqueline Conciatore.
Title: Navigating filter bubbles / Jacqueline Conciatore Senter.
Description: New York : Cavendish Square, 2019. | Series:
News literacy | Includes glossary and index.
Identifiers: ISBN 9781502641311 (pbk.) | ISBN 9781502641328
(library bound) | ISBN 9781502641335 (ebook)
Subjects: LCSH: Information filtering systems--Juvenile literature.
| Web browsing--Psychological aspects--Juvenile literature. |
Internet searching--Psychological aspects--Juvenile literature.
| Content analysis (Communication)--Juvenile literature.
Classification: LCC Z667.6 S46 2019 | DDC 025.04--dc23

Editorial Director: David McNamara
Editor: Caitlyn Miller
Copy Editor: Lisa Goldstein
Associate Art Director: Alan Sliwinski
Designer: Joe Parenteau
Production Coordinator: Karol Szymczuk
Photo Research: J8 Media

Printed in the United States of America

CONTENTS

Filter bubbles can cause internet users to fall out of touch with diverse experiences and challenging viewpoints.

Influential Gatekeepers

Before the internet—before Snapchat, Instagram and YouTube—our relationship with the news was much different. Although there were far fewer news media choices, people set aside time to keep up with the news. The primary news sources were newspapers and TV news broadcasts. People trusted the news and had faith in the reporters and anchors on television. In fact, the most popular newsman in the United States from 1962 until 1981, Walter Cronkite, was known as "the most trusted man in America."

There's a big difference between then and now. In 1976, 72 percent of Americans said in a Gallup poll that they had a "great deal/fair amount" of trust in mass media (newspapers, TV, radio, magazines). By 2016, that figure had fallen to 32 percent.

Television news anchor Walter Cronkite was known as the most trusted man in America.

Before the internet, entertainment brought people together. Television was the most popular form of entertainment, and many people watched the same shows. The most-watched TV episode ever, excluding any Super Bowl game, aired in 1983. It was the final episode of *M*A*S*H*, a series about a US Korean War hospital. More than 100 million people watched that series finale. No show (excepting sports and presidential debates) has come close to that number of viewers since.

Different people and groups have always had different opinions of America, based on unique experiences. But, prior to the internet, many people relied on the same sources to form opinions about issues—and to make decisions about important matters such as who to vote for. Quite literally, most people were reading from the same page.

The Internet and World Wide Web

In the 1990s, along came the internet. The internet is the system of connected computers that provides the menu of shows, videos, games, social media and other content on the World Wide Web. Right away, many people saw that the internet could unite people in a way that had never been possible. Today that unity is still a goal, and this ability to unify still exists. Nonetheless, the public seems more divided than ever. There are many reasons for the divisions. However, some people blame the internet, at least in part,

In the 1970s and 1980s, more people watched the same television programs, such as *M*A*S*H*.

for channeling people into like-minded groups, cliques, and tribes. There are even digital versions of mobs.

It doesn't seem like people are reading from the same page anymore. Often people on different sides of the political divide—liberals versus conservatives, Republicans versus Democrats—don't agree even about basic facts. Sometimes, it can feel like different groups are living in different realities.

For a democracy to function, people must have a common starting point, a shared sense of what's true. From that common base of information and knowledge, people can debate and grapple with questions about how society should be governed. But in some ways our windows on the world are growing more individualized and isolated.

Digital intermediaries, or go-betweens, known as online filters, are part of the problem. They can lead to a situation known as the filter bubble.

What Is a Filter Bubble?

A filter bubble is not a physical thing you can see or touch. Rather, it is an effect of technology and a way of being in the world. When we say someone is "in a bubble," we mean that he or she sees a unique reality. There is a big world out there, but the person in the bubble experiences only what's inside the membrane of that bubble.

Filter bubbles are indirectly formed by the services and platforms people use online. Google and Facebook are prime examples. These companies use algorithms, or codes that make choices, to control what the user sees. An algorithm filters out the stuff it decides a user won't like, based on his or her past behavior online. This data

Many people argue that filter bubbles threaten democracy because voters no longer share the same information base.

includes websites visited, games bought online, and ads clicked on. In addition to shaping a user's experience on the web, filter bubbles can influence his or her ideas of what's going on in the world. Filter bubbles then shape that person's opinions on important issues.

The History of Filter Bubbles

The concept of filter bubbles is relatively new. It arose as a much-discussed topic in 2011 after an activist named Eli Pariser gave a talk on the web called "Beware Online 'Filter Bubbles.'" The video talk went viral and suddenly a lot of people were discussing filter bubbles.

But it wasn't until just after the 2016 election—when many people were in shock that Donald Trump had been elected president—that filter bubbles really became an idea and problem that people thought and

Eli Pariser brought filter bubbles to public attention.

talked about. How could most news reporters have missed the signs that many people were planning to vote for the controversial Trump? Why were Americans so angry and divided? Were filter bubbles one answer to these questions?

People began talking more about filter bubbles after Donald Trump was elected president of the United States.

The Effects on Democracy

When it comes to filter bubbles, the concern that most people focus on is the health of democracy. As citizens, we all face big questions. How much should each person pay in taxes? Should rich people pay a bigger share of taxes than poor people? How should society punish criminals? Should society give certain criminals a second chance? Should it be legal for ordinary citizens to own and carry guns? If so, what kinds of guns? Hunting weapons or assault rifles? These are just some of the thousands of questions people in a democracy decide.

As a group, voters answer these questions at the ballot box, when they vote for president, members of Congress, and state and local legislators.

ANXIETY ABOUT TECHNOLOGY IS NOT NEW

Worry about filter bubbles reflects anxiety about the ways technology affects society. Throughout history, new technologies often have caused a significant amount of concern. Some worries prove to be less reasonable than others. For example, when people in Victorian England fell in love with the novel, critics complained that readers, especially women, would become "overexcited," which was an undesirable state. Some worried the women readers wouldn't be able to separate fact from fantasy.

Blogger Shane Parrish wrote: "Each new technology brings with it a whole host of costs and benefits. Many are realized only as time passes. The invention of books led people to worry that memory and oral tradition would erode. Paper caused panic as young people switched from slates to this newfangled medium."

This doesn't mean that all anxieties about technology are without basis. Most people agree that the popularity of television had huge impacts on society. For one thing, TV cut into the time people spent socializing with extended families and friends. In much the same way, cell phones have drastically changed the way people communicate.

Many people say filter bubbles stop people from having all the information needed to make wise decisions as citizens, like when they vote.

It's very difficult for people in a society to decide on these critical issues if they don't agree on the same facts or see all sides of an argument. Many people say filter bubbles stop people from having all the information needed to make wise decisions as citizens. At first glance, it might not seem to matter much that web users are increasingly viewing different online content. However, many experts argue that it matters very much. Our democracy is at stake, they say.

Deepening Divides

Online filters "reward" web users with content they like. They do this because people usually prefer to read information that confirms what they think about the world. Someone who loved the latest *Star Wars* movie doesn't necessarily want to spend time watching a YouTube video about how terrible it was. Online filters "know" this about human beings. Therefore, they give us what we want to see and read about. The problem comes when citizens miss key news stories because of filter bubbles. For example, what if a voter's favorite senator did something wrong, and she misses that news because it didn't come up on the top of her Facebook feed? Without access to this news, the voter can't understand why people are suddenly speaking out against that senator. She believes the senator is a great woman. The voter becomes angry and confused. She wonders why the senator's opponents are so irrational. This is how filter bubbles contribute to the increasing divisiveness we're seeing in the world.

Personal Impacts

Critics argue that filter bubbles have negative personal impacts too. By removing information from our field of

People in society have become more divided about politics. Some experts blame filter bubbles. Here, two men argue at a protest after the 2016 election.

BARACK OBAMA ON SOCIAL BUBBLES

During a farewell address to the nation after completing his second presidential term in 2016, Barack Obama discussed the problem of social bubbles:

> [We] retreat into our own bubbles, whether in our neighborhoods or on college campuses, or places of worship, or especially our social media feeds, surrounded by people who look like us and share the same political outlook and never challenge our assumptions ... And increasingly, we become so secure in our bubbles that we start accepting only information, whether it's true or not, that fits our opinions, instead of basing our opinions on the evidence that is out there.

In other words, Obama is saying that bubbles exist in the real world and online. The effect is the same in both places. When trapped in a bubble, people make poorly informed decisions. These decisions can have a major impact. That's why it is so important to be aware of social bubbles—and fight them.

vision that may conflict with our world views, filter bubbles harm our growth as critical thinkers. Critical thinking involves answering questions using logic and reason. It requires having all the facts. Without the ability to think critically, people may make poor decisions. These decisions include those at the voting booth and also big, personal, life decisions. For example, critical thinking skills are necessary when selecting a doctor or choosing a career.

Furthermore, when websites and social media spoon-feed only content that makes users feel good, users are more likely to rapidly click here, there, and everywhere. Their attention is fractured. They may fall out of the habit of concentrating on fewer topics and thinking about those matters more deeply. "Personalized filters play to the most compulsive parts of you ... to get you to click things more," says filter bubbles expert Eli Pariser.

Filter bubbles also limit our ability to handle the complexities of the world. Life is far more interesting when the universe tosses in a few challenges. Or, as Pariser says: "A world constructed from the familiar is the world in which there's nothing to learn."

In addition, when we overcome challenges, we feel good about ourselves. We grow in confidence and we move on to the next challenge. This allows us to move through life as well-functioning people. Confronting ideas and information that makes us uncomfortable is just the type of challenge we need to live life fully.

Filter bubbles have "turned out to be more of a problem than I, or many others, would have expected," said Bill Gates.

Explaining Filter Bubbles

As we've seen, search engines and social media sites such as Facebook use algorithms to filter content. This means they give users some content but leave out other content. The information bubbles that can result are worrisome—not only because web users may miss important arguments in a debate or content that completes a picture, but because they may get misleading, inaccurate, or even outright false content. One of the world's most famous technology leaders, Bill Gates, spoke about this very issue in 2017: "Do people really want to be in a [bubble] where the facts are wrong? Because over time, wrong facts don't lead to good things. If you're hearing 'Don't use vaccines,' or about drug side effects

Social media platforms like Snapchat can create filter bubbles.

that are false, that's not good for you." Filter bubbles have "turned out to be more of a problem than I, or many others, would have expected," Gates said.

Filter bubbles have defining characteristics. Learning about these characteristics can help you recognize them. In this chapter, we'll also look at how filters work on leading platforms, including Google, Snapchat, Facebook, Twitter, YouTube, and Instagram.

Filters Are Necessary

The web is vast. Each time you enter keywords in its search box, Google must scan a sea of information. In fact, Google scans not one billion or even one hundred billion web pages with each search, Google's algorithm combs through hundreds of billions of web pages.

But it's even bigger than that. When you perform a Google search, you are not searching the entire web. You are only searching Google's *index* of the web. The web outside of Google's index is in fact much larger (but also includes many dead pages, those ones with the "404" errors). In November 2016, Google said it knew of 130 trillion distinct pages. That figure refers to the number of distinct URLs on the web.

These numbers are hard to imagine, but the point is that web users need filters. Without them, we would never be able to find anything specific except by sheer luck.

As you probably know, even individual websites require search filters. The *Washington Post*, for example, publishes more than 1,200 news stories, videos, and graphic items such as charts and maps, per day. If someone doesn't want to just browse through the *Post*, and is looking for something specific, he or she uses the search bar. Search filters and filtering algorithms make quick searches possible. They give people what they need, and fast. According to Google, its searches take less than a second.

Am I in a Bubble?

If you use social media such as Snapchat, Reddit, Facebook, Google and any of the other popular services and platforms, you're probably in a filter bubble. That is, internet users are likely in filter bubbles if they don't take steps to avoid filters or the effects of filters. These methods include using anti-tracking software or actively seeking out a variety of content, people, or groups to follow.

The fact that people even have to wonder if they are in bubbles shows one key characteristic of filters: we can't see them. Anyone who searches for, say, "virtual reality games" on Google, doesn't know what items in the Google search are being filtered out. A user who seeks out YouTube videos for "gun control," doesn't know what videos are outside his or her bubble.

We can't see the filters at work. They are mysterious. Even people who study and think about filtering algorithms don't know exactly how the algorithms make their "decisions."

Algorithms help businesses such as Google and Facebook and Amazon put "targeted" ads and other content in front of you. This means content that is specifically tailored to you based on your past online behavior. Algorithms can give these businesses an advantage over other businesses. That's why algorithms are secret.

Personalization of content helps companies such as Amazon give users ads and other content they might like.

"Neither Facebook nor Google nor Pinterest explains the intricacies of its code," said *Washington Post* reporter Caitlin Dewey in a 2015 article. "Even though algorithms arguably shape how we think and what we know, no one gets to open them up and see how they work."

Many people don't know about filter bubbles or filtering algorithms. One study in 2015 found that more than 62.5 percent of Facebook users were not even aware that Facebook hid some stories from its news feeds. The Facebook users just assumed everything their friends posted would show up in their feeds.

It's All About You

Perhaps *the* defining characteristic of filter bubbles is a trend known as personalization. It is a main goal of filters. Algorithms work to give you what you most want to see. To achieve this goal, algorithms collect data about you. This data includes your browsing history, search history, and click data (what you click on first, for example). They also use information such as your location, social media connections, and even what kind of computer you're using.

There is a great deal of additional personal information people give to Facebook and other services that also goes into the data banks. Things like where they live, what music they like, what movies they like, foods they eat, clothes they wear, places they've been, events they plan to attend ... and much, much more.

Companies say that personalization helps them provide targeted content. These companies aim to provide news, GIFs, videos, posts, and memes that web users really like. There is one other important reason for personalization: advertising. All that data allows advertisers to reach individual customers more effectively with ads. Information about users' browsing histories, searches, and more is valuable to Google and social media platforms.

Personalization technology makes finding things online easier, but there also are costs related to this method. Many people worry about privacy, because online businesses collect so much information. For example, Google has said it mines the content of emails to provide "personally relevant product features," while Amazon tracks the passages that customers highlight in the Kindle e-readers.

Says Pariser in his book *The Filter Bubble*:

> When you read books on your Kindle, the data about which phrases you highlight, which pages you turn, and whether you read straight through or skip around are all fed back into Amazon's servers and can be used to indicate what books you might like next. When you log in after a day reading Kindle e-books at the beach, Amazon can subtly customize its site to appeal to what you've read: If you've spent a lot of time with the latest James Patterson, but only glanced at that new diet guide, you might see more commercial thrillers and fewer health books.

Another cost has to do with the quality of information personalized feeds provide. It's human nature to click on more extreme kinds of stories, images, memes and videos. Content about people behaving badly, committing crimes, or having public meltdowns generally receive more clicks. After a user clicks on these over-the-top stories, the algorithms feed that kind of content back to the user even more. That's because our clicks help determine what we see.

President Obama warned young people of these dangers, during a speech at Hampton University in 2010:

> You're coming of age in a 24/7 media environment that bombards us with all kinds of content and exposes us to all kinds of

Barack Obama has warned young voters to pay attention to bubbles online and in the real world.

arguments, some of which don't always rank that high on the truth meter. And with iPods and iPads; and Xboxes and PlayStations—none of which I know how to work—information becomes a distraction, a diversion, a form of entertainment, rather than a tool of empowerment, rather than the means of emancipation. So all of this is not only putting pressure on you; it's putting new pressure on our country and on our democracy.

It is a common experience to go online looking for certain information. But when doing an online search, the web user often gets sucked into silly or distracting content for thirty minutes or even longer. A lot of web users love cute or funny animal videos, after all. Learning to navigate filter bubbles and avoid the easy distractions of personalized content can help users stay in control of how they spend their time.

Breaking It Down

Let's break down filter bubbles by service or social media application.

Facebook

At one time, everything friends posted appeared on users' Facebook "walls." But eventually the sheer number of posts led Facebook to phase out that system. By 2011, Facebook was personalizing news items so that the news it thought would most interest a user appeared at the top

The posts users see at the top of the Facebook feeds are the results of the workings of a complex algorithm.

of that user's feed. The algorithm considers hundreds of variables to decide what a person will prefer, *Slate*'s Will Oremus reported. And the algorithm doesn't just figure out if you'll like something, Oremus wrote in 2016:

> It doesn't just predict whether you'll actually hit the like button on a post based on your past behavior. It also predicts whether you'll click, comment, share, or hide it, or even mark it as spam. It will predict each of these outcomes, and others, with a certain degree of confidence, then combine them all to produce a single relevancy score that's specific to both you and that post. Once every possible post in your feed has received its relevancy score, the sorting algorithm can put them in the order that you'll

see them on the screen. The post you see at the top of your feed, then, has been chosen over thousands of others as the one most likely to make you laugh, cry, smile, click, like, share, or comment.

In other words, Facebook's algorithm considers a huge amount of information about users. This allows Facebook to feed its users the most appealing content possible. Facebook wants people to keep coming back, to stay on the site as long as possible, and to share posts widely. The algorithm is designed to keep us hooked.

Instagram

Instagram announced it would start filtering content in March 2016. "You may be surprised to learn that people

Instagram, a photo-sharing site, started personalizing content in 2016. After that change, users no longer saw posts in the order they were posted.

miss on average 70 percent of their feeds," the company said in a blog post when it announced the change. "As Instagram has grown, it's become harder to keep up with all the photos and videos people share. This means you often don't see the posts you might care about the most." To address this problem, Instagram adopted an algorithm that ordered the posts in a feed based on

- likes;
- the relationship between the person with the Instagram account and whoever posted an image; and
- how recently the post was made.

Twitter

In some ways, Twitter *is* a filter bubble, because you choose who to follow and can instantly mute or block anyone with whom you disagree. In 2016, social scientists led by psychologist William Brady of New York University released a study that showed how content travels within Twitter

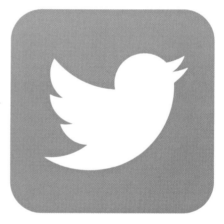

On Twitter, it's very easy to mute or otherwise avoid opinions we find disagreeable.

filter bubbles. The study looked at tweets that talked about political issues such as gun control or climate change. It found that tweets with "moral-emotional" words (for example, a tweet claiming someone was acting out of greed, or accusing an idea or policy of being evil) increased the chance of a tweet being shared. But users only shared the moral and emotional tweets with people who tended to agree with their opinions. For the most part, people with different views didn't see these tweets.

YouTube

YouTube's algorithm determines much of the content you see, including "recommended" videos and which selection of its billions of videos will be "up next." The site has been successful at keeping people hooked. In fact, every day people across the world watch more than one billion hours of video on the site. Despite its popularity, YouTube, which is owned by Google, has come under criticism. It appears the algorithm has been promoting videos that are violent and material that tends to cause arguments between

YouTube, like other platforms, uses filtering algorithms designed to keep people coming back.

groups of people. According to a report by the *Wall Street Journal*, the algorithm "often leads users to channels that feature conspiracy theories, political viewpoints and misleading videos, even when those users haven't shown interest in such content."

Snapchat

In 2018, Snapchat announced an algorithm that would order items according to "personal relevance," rather than in order of time posted. Many Snapchat users were not happy. When celebrity Kylie Jenner tweeted, "Sooo does anyone else not open Snapchat anymore? Or is it just me... ugh this is so sad," the company's stock value fell sharply. A couple of weeks later, Snapchat laid off 120 engineers. There were factors besides Jenner's tweet, but some people said her words were no help for the company that has been struggling with competitors. Snapchat appears to be sticking to its new look. The company did report that downloads of the Snapchat app were up, despite complaints. One lesson here is that the public, at least those who are aware of algorithms, often resent the lack of control they have over their favorite social media apps.

Bubbles, Bubbles Everywhere

Some people argue that filters don't present a real barrier to diversity of information. They say that Google search results don't differ that heavily by user and point to studies that back up this claim. Others, including Facebook founder Mark Zuckerberg, say that Facebook presents users a far greater range of information than traditional media like newspapers ever did:

Even if a lot of your friends come from the same kind of background or have the same political or religious beliefs, if you know a couple of hundred people, there's a good chance that even maybe a small percent, maybe 5% or 10% or 15% of them will have different viewpoints, which means that their perspectives are now going to be shown in your news feed.

And if you compare that to traditional media where people will typically pick a newspaper or a TV station that they want to watch and just get 100% of the view from that, people are actually getting exposed to much more different kinds of content through social media than they would have otherwise or have been in the past.

Other critics of the concept of filter bubbles point to human nature. They say that even where the bubble effects seem strongest—where divisions are most

Facebook founder Mark Zuckerberg has said filter bubbles are not as big a problem as many people make them out to be.

obvious—the problem is not necessarily an algorithm. The problem, they believe, is that humans will also seek out information that confirms their beliefs. Especially on Twitter, people search for members of their own "tribes." Users follow those with opinions they like, tweets they approve of and points of view they value.

Mills Baker, a product design manager for the question-and-answer website Quora, said:

> I wouldn't follow my crazy uncle on Twitter; instead, I follow journalists, celebrities, and some friends whose tweets I like and whom I generally admire and find interesting. If someone we follow on Twitter shares something that offends us, we often mute or unfollow them.

The problem, Baker argues, is that people naturally prefer to be in bubbles. Blaming algorithms for our bubbles is wrong because it prevents people from taking responsibility, he says. But even on Twitter the self-filtering isn't a problem, he argues. Baker says that people get plenty of ideas opposite from their own just by following the debates. And on Twitter, there is no doubt that people do debate. When you participate in or follow the threads in an argument, you're getting many different opinions, Baker claims.

Since we do tend to prefer people and posts that confirm our opinions and world views, it's useful to guard against bubbles in any form—online and in the real world.

IT'S JUST CODE

Some people argue that filter bubbles aren't new at all. When people relied only on newspapers and local TV news, there were people behind the scenes deciding what stories to publish and which should lead the evening broadcast.

But that system was different than today's filtering. For one thing, at that time, everyone knew what the filter was. It was an editor behind a desk whose job was to make sure the newspaper reported the most important news. It was a producer at the TV station working with reporters to decide which stories would air. For another thing, more people were getting more of the same information. After all, there is only one *LA Times,* one *Chicago Tribune,* one *Sarasota Herald-Tribune.*

There was one other difference too. Newspapers and other news organizations had (and many still have) employees whose only job is to represent readers. These "ombudsmen" investigate and report when the company makes a mistake. Here's an example: In the 1990s, *Washington Post* reporter Janet Cooke wrote a story about an eight-year-old boy named Jimmy who was addicted to heroin. The story was widely read and ultimately won journalism's biggest award, a Pulitzer Prize. Then it was discovered that Cooke, under pressure to produce hard-hitting journalism and wanting a big story, had made the whole thing up. That's when the ombudsman stepped in, who was a veteran journalist named Bill Green. Green wrote a lengthy piece about how the *Post* got things so wrong. (The *Post* returned the Pulitzer Prize.)

Although social media companies like Facebook do feel some sense of responsibility to their users, they usually have no office or role like the independent ombudsman. When Facebook was accused of allowing fake news posts to course through people's news feeds and sway the 2016 presidential election, it was the CEO Mark Zuckerberg himself who responded.

Summing Up

Given its vastness, the web wouldn't be very useful to us without any filtering at all. But services such as Google and platforms such as Facebook are relying more than ever on filtering technology to give us increasingly personalized information. To make this personalization possible, web users generally give up a lot of personal data. Data collection methods raise concerns about privacy. In addition, personalized content isn't generally high-quality content. It's often superficial, feeding into our natural tendencies to want to be entertained instead of educated and enlightened.

Not everyone agrees that filter bubble effects are big enough to shape people's sense of events or harden their existing beliefs (by reinforcing the same ideas over and over). Remember, filter bubbles are a new problem, and society is still trying to understand them. However, there are solutions.

Sharing a wide range of information and opinions is the best way to balance out the effects of filter bubbles.

Fighting Filter Bubbles

nstead of shared information, more and more, we have separate universes of personalized content. Eli Pariser calls this "the web of one." Just as it is a citizen's democratic duty to stay informed about current events, perhaps it is a citizen's duty to break out of our information cocoons. Luckily, there are a lot of ways to break out of filter bubbles. These solutions fall under two categories: tech solutions and personal solutions.

Tech Solutions

Clear Your Browsing History, Cache, and Cookies

It's helpful to take the steps necessary to clear browsing data, cache, and cookies. When you do, algorithms do not have as much data with which to personalize your feeds and results. You can set your browser to clear your history and cache every time you sign off.

When you clear your computer cache, you clear instructions or other data the computer has stored to perform repeated actions (such as loading a web page) faster. (Pages may load more slowly as a result.)

Additionally, you can set your browsers to disable cookies. Cookies are also known as "web cookies" or "browser cookies." These are small files that help websites track user activity, such as which items someone looks at when visiting a shopping site. At times, disabling cookies can interfere with loading some websites (which may then ask you to enable cookies). Experiment with different settings and see how the changes work for you.

Enable "Do Not Track" Settings and Searching Incognito

In the Google Chrome browser's "privacy and security" settings, choose the option to "Send a 'Do Not Track' request with your browsing traffic." This measure is no guarantee, and when you click the button you'll see that. A pop-up box will appear and explain that enabling "Do Not Track" means that a "do not track request" will be triggered whenever you browse. However, the pop-up box also says, "Any effect depends on whether a website responds to the request, and how the request is interpreted."

The browsers Chrome, Firefox, Edge, Opera, and Internet Explorer all offer the opportunity to browse the web "incognito" or "in

Many browsers give users the option to browse the web "incognito."

private." This option allows users to browse the web without triggering the algorithms that track data, store cookies, and more. This doesn't mean Google can't track you at all. That said, browsing incognito is a step most experts recommend to tackle filter bubbles.

Try Different Search Engines, Apps, Extensions, and Plug-Ins

Some search engines, most notably DuckDuckGo, sell themselves in the marketplace as browsers that won't track your activity. Another browser like this is StartPage. Similarly, there are many tools and websites designed to help people move outside their filter bubbles.

AllSides (http://www.allsides.com) is a website and news service with a mission to "free people from filter bubbles so they can better understand the world and each other." It offers the same news stories from politically

Search engine DuckDuckGo doesn't track users' online activity the way other search engines do.

different angles and offers a school program designed to teach students about media bias and civil discussions. Its program, called Mismatch, pairs students around the United States who have different political perspectives in "respectful video conversations."

Another valuable tool is Read Across the Aisle (http://www.readacrosstheaisle.com), which bills itself as a "Fitbit for your filter bubble." It tells you the political leaning of specific stories. Read Across the Aisle's Chrome extension tells you how much time you've spent reading news, what your bias is, and what your most-viewed site is. The iOS app will nudge you, like a Fitbit, to read more diverse sources if it detects a pattern of reading inside a bubble.

Fiskkit (http://www.fiskkit.com) is "where everyone can share and discuss news stories based on facts and logic." The site allows you to share articles that you've tagged with fixed labels ("not supported," "matter of opinion," "funny") and to comment, sharing your opinions and insights about the article. Articles with enough tags get ratings.

Finally, Escape Your Bubble (http://www.escapeyour bubble.com) is a Chrome extension that will insert posts in your Facebook news feed that represent different takes on issues. If you're a Democrat looking to better understand Republicans, for example, the service will insert posts highlighting "the positive aspects of those you wish to understand and be more accepting of." The goal is to promote a greater sense of understanding of opposing viewpoints. According to the Escape Your Bubble team, "You'll learn to understand and accept thy fellow countrymen."

Use Library Computers

Most libraries have computer work stations where filter bubbles should not be a factor. Personalization isn't possible on a computer shared by scores of people every day. (If you log into a personal account, for example, your Google or Facebook account, then filtering is again at

Using library computers is an effective way of fighting filter bubbles.

work.) Working at the library has a bonus. It gets you out of another bubble: your house!

Personal Solutions

You may find that simply being more aware of online personalization effects will cause you to search differently and read your social media feeds with more of an eye for bias. Here are some other tips:

Read Several Sources of News and Information

There are many sources of information and news, and these sources come in different formats. Listening to podcasts is a great addition to your Facebook, Tumblr, or Snapchat feeds. However, relying solely on social media for news is not the best practice. (If you do rely on social media for news, know you're not alone. A Pew Research Center and Knight Foundation study found that more than 40 percent of all US adults get their news from Facebook.)

News sites for young people include Smithsonian's Tween Tribune and the *New York Times* Learning Network. Youth Radio offers a lot of great stories that you can both read and listen to online. Some of the stories found there include, "I'm A Cheerleader, Here's Why I Take A Knee," "GenZ Fashion: From YouTube to Your Closet," and "Teen Snowboarder Chloe Kim Wins Olympic Gold."

Have a Nourishing Media Diet

In an article for Medium about how to read the news in high school, journalist Jihii Jolly suggests that young people try to develop good news habits early. Look to a variety of sources to avoid the bubble, she says. Her own media diet is as follows:

> In the morning: Read the *NYT Morning Briefing* and *NY Today* on my phone using the NYTNow App ...
>
> At work: I subscribe to about 35 e-mail newsletters from different news organizations and bloggers that filter into a "News" folder in my inbox. I'll sift through them over the day, read short things and save the long-stuff for later.
>
> On the train home: I'm tired of looking at the computer or phone so I'll listen to a podcast episode or an NPR show.
>
> At home: I don't have TV so I'll watch a newscast from the Reuters TV App, which lets you select the length of your newscast and personalizes it for you, or the app Watchup, which is similar but aggregates sources. Or, I'll watch videos that I've saved from *Vice/NYT/* the *Guardian* and various other news channels on YouTube.

While she does consume a lot of media, her news diet demonstrates how breaking out of filter bubbles requires a focused effort.

Fact-Check

Sometimes the problem is about more than a sea of slanted news. Sometimes news that is entirely made up— fake news—will sneak into social media feeds. It is widely believed that many fake news stories today come from

Russia. In fact, a US government investigation reported that the Russian government has repeatedly tried to influence American election outcomes. Russian bots, automated computer programs, tweet or post to Facebook extreme stories designed to get people angry about important issues.

Other fake news appears during the election season, created by people who want their candidate to win. They make up stories designed to influence people to vote for one candidate over another. An example is a story a young Republican named Cameron Harris made up just before the 2016 presidential election. He claimed that there were tens of thousands of votes in fake ballot boxes in an Ohio warehouse. He wanted to feed rumors being stoked at the time by candidate Donald Trump that the election would be "rigged." He was suggesting that Hillary Clinton could only win if the election was "rigged," that is, if she had somehow cheated. Once Harris posted the story, it blazed "across the web like some kind of counterfeit comet," said the New York Times:

> The ballot box story, promoted by a half-dozen Facebook pages Mr. Harris had created for the purpose, flew around the web, fueled by indignant comments from people who were certain that Mrs. Clinton was going to cheat Mr. Trump of victory and who welcomed the proof. It was eventually shared with six million people, according to CrowdTangle, which tracks web audiences.

BUBBLES IN EVERYDAY LIFE

Being limited because of bubbles is not just a problem in the online world. Most of us are in some kind of bubble on a day-to-day basis. Bubbles can be like safety zones. We're familiar with what's inside them and so we often stay there.

For example, kids tend to make friends largely with other kids who are like them—those who live in the same neighborhoods or have the same interests. Some kids may even feel dislike for kids from other groups. Cliques are not only hurtful; they also limit our experiences. Without reaching beyond our comfort zones, life becomes pretty, well, lifeless. Think about the plots of most movies and books. They are generally about people being forced outside of their bubbles. The *Harry Potter* series is one example. In each book in the series, Harry is confronted with new challenges, starting with going to Hogwarts School, then learning to rely on his own knowledge of and skill in magic and ending with his battle against the evil Lord Voldemort.

It's worth keeping an eye on your own day-to-day filter bubble, just to make sure you pull yourself away from your comfort zone every now and then.

Despite people's efforts to promote fake news, there are methods for separating fact and fiction. One important and easy method is to look at the URL or website address associated with the story. Stories from abcnews.com will be legitimately from that network. However, stories from ABCnews.com.co, for example, are not legitimate. Likewise, stories from Bloomberg.ma are trying to seem like they come from Bloomberg.com, which is a popular site for business news.

Remember the World Is Big

Make it a point to seek out people on social media as friends or people to follow who are outside of your bubble. Visit diverse kinds of sites and research new topics. If you do decide to expose yourself to opposite political views, according to experts, it can be important to go gently at first. Someone who is, for example, very much in favor of gun control won't want to dive in to read the NRA's news feed right away. Rather, try to find moderate (middle of the road) voices on issues, they advise. The wonderful thing is that once you start widening your reading habits, the personalization of your filter bubble will get broader too.

Seek Media Literacy

Being smart and savvy about what you read online will help you fight the problems of division and disinformation. If you see someone sharing a story on Snapchat that you suspect is false, point out the possibility. When people flag fake news, they are taking an important step in the fight against misinformation. Because fake news wants to create division, it is often the most damaging content out there. Strive for media literacy!

Make a Commitment to Civility

While you're building your media literacy skills, make it a point to reject any kind of negative, hateful or bullying talk. When a person in a debate or argument about issues resorts to insulting the person they're communicating with, it's called an ad hominem attack. It literally means "to the person." Ad hominem attacks are not acceptable because they are not relevant. "Your shoes are ugly," has nothing to do with gun control, right? When someone makes an ad hominem attack, that person is showing weakness in his or her ability to argue a point. Ad hominem attacks are never a legitimate point of debate. If you remember this point, you can keep many future debates on the right track.

You might even want to consider learning about nonviolent communication. The organization Play in the

Media literacy skills help us to communicate responsibly.

PLAY A GAME

"From fake news to chaos! How bad are you? Get as many followers as you can." So reads the welcome page of a new game designed to protect people against the persuasive effects of fake news and disinformation. The Bad News game (http://www.getbadnews.com) is an online challenge meant to help people better recognize fake news.

By playing a "master of disinformation" online, you seek to drum up lots of Twitter followers by sharing fake news, emotional memes and headlines, inciting fear, attacking large institutions such as the government and attacking individuals who criticize your content. The game walks you through choices, all designed to stir up emotions and expand your Twitter base. Along the way you earn badges named after different methods of disinformation: polarization, impersonation, conspiracy theories, discrediting those who disagree with you, and trolling. The goal is to get as many Twitter followers as possible.

The Bad News game was developed by researchers at the University of Cambridge and a Dutch media group called Drog. You may want to tell your teacher about the Bad News game, because the site includes a guide for teachers about using the game.

Wild! defines nonviolent communication as "a lifelong commitment to seeing beyond differences." Play in the Wild! offers programs designed to help students deal with conflict respectfully and productively.

Pay Attention to Your Real-World Bubbles

Critics of the filter bubble concept often point out that filter bubbles were a problem long before the internet and that people choose to be in filter bubbles in the real world as well as online. We make friends with like-minded people, live near others like us, and go to the same movies and music concerts. In other words, *we* are the problem, not technology. It is true that we prefer the familiar over the strange, and we find comfort being with others like ourselves, who think like we do and like the same things we do. Pay attention to your real-world bubbles and see if you can add some change and variety to your social circles as well as your online circles. Remember this quote attributed to the ancient biographer Plutarch: "I don't need a friend who changes when I change and who nods when I nod; my shadow does that much better."

Halfway There Already

Clearly there are many different steps people can take to burst through their filter bubbles—bubbles that are online and those in the real world. The biggest step of all is one readers of this book have already taken—developing awareness. Many people don't even know about online filters. Without that knowledge they can't possibly be on the lookout for bubble effects. Knowing is half the battle.

Bobby Ray Simmons Jr. (rap artist B.o.B) says he believes Earth is flat. Filter bubbles encourage false views like these.

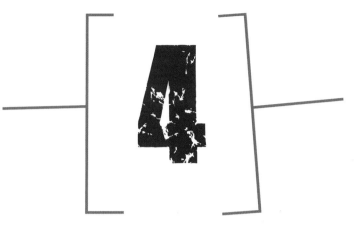

A Strange Case

Filter bubbles can lead to echo chambers, which are little universes of repeated ideas. In echo chambers, people push the same (sometimes questionable) facts, ideas, and arguments over and over again. Some say that echo chambers make people more strongly attached to their beliefs and trick them into thinking more people agree with them than actually do. In other words, echo chambers can cause us to believe everyone thinks as we do.

The statements of celebrities can especially go viral and start bouncing around within echo chambers. This includes even the strangest statements, such as tweets by Bobby Ray Simmons Jr. (the rap artist known as B.o.B) that Earth is flat. (Another celebrity who says he believes this is NBA star Kyrie Irving.)

The flat Earth movement is a good case study for understanding filter bubbles—and everything that is wrong with filter bubbles. There have always been people here and there who believe Earth is flat. Only a few times has the idea gained real popularity with the public, though the idea was popular with just a small portion of the public. Once was in the nineteenth century, and now it has picked up steam again. Google Trends show a definite path upward, beginning in 2016, for the search phrase "flat Earth." (This means that more people began doing Google searches for "flat Earth" in 2016.) The science website *Clean Technica* reported in February 2018 that "a recent article about the Flat Earth Society claiming the launch of the Falcon Heavy was faked was one of the most widely read stories on *Clean Technica* in its entire history, with lots of people [fiercely] supporting the notion that the world is indeed flat."

Physicist Neil deGrasse Tyson speaks out against false ideas and theories.

It's likely that filter bubbles played a role in this sudden upswing in the flat Earth movement. People including Simmons have gotten into public Twitter arguments with leading physicist Neil deGrasse Tyson, and the news media has covered these Twitter debates. The news media also gives attention to celebrities simply for saying they believe Earth is flat.

In the past, people with ideas that have been scientifically disproved were mostly isolated. But thanks to social media, individuals now have access to thousands of people who share their ideas. According to the *New York Times*, a Facebook group called "Flat Earth — No Trolls" has 22,538 members. People in this group, the *Times* says, share "unscientific evidence that the world was indeed flat and mocked 'globers' who claimed otherwise."

It's not clear how many people who claim to follow the movement are doing so as a joke. But at least some people are just having fun with this disproved theory.

If an idea as outrageous as flat Earth can gain popularity thanks in part to social media and online bubbles, imagine how easy it can be to fall into that trap with more complex issues or questions—issues such as climate change, whether vaccines are safe, and whether crime is up or down. These issues may indeed have clear answers and fact trails that point to clear conclusions, but they are certainly more complicated than the question of whether Earth is flat.

The unwelcome fact is that false information— news that really is fake—can travel more easily than the truth. A study of Twitter that was published in *Science* in March 2018 found that, "False news reached more people than the truth; the top 1% of false news cascades [spread] to between 1000 and 100,000 people, whereas the truth rarely [spread] to more than 1000 people."

Flat Earthers claim that the government guards the edges of Earth to keep people from falling off the edge.

One reason fake news travels more readily is that it tends to be more interesting. Fake news is often more outrageous, shocking, and just plain entertaining. "False stories inspired fear, disgust, and surprise in replies, true stories inspired anticipation, sadness, joy, and trust," the study said.

Many people blame Twitter bots for the spread of fake news. But the researchers found this wasn't the case. "Contrary to conventional wisdom, robots accelerated the spread of true and false news at the same rate, [suggesting] that false news spreads more than the truth because humans, not robots, are more likely to spread it."

The good news is you can avoid filter bubbles and fake news, whether it's from a bot or not. Research has shown that even a brief introduction to concepts related to media literacy (like filter bubbles, fake news, and clickbait) can "inoculate" young people against the misleading nature of such content. In other words, if you are aware of the problem, you already have a head start.

Solutions

It isn't that hard to avoid the effects of filter bubbles, especially when it comes to conspiracy theories like the flat Earth theories. (Flat Earth is a conspiracy theory because its believers argue that the government hides the truth from us. Some "flat Earthers," for example, claim that the government guards the edges of Antarctica to keep people from falling off the edge of Earth.) The key is to make sure you seek out a variety of information sources. There are some great science resources for young people. Check out How Stuff Works, Bill Nye, PBS Kids, and *Science News for Kids*. NOVA is a rich site full of amazing and extremely interesting science videos. The Exploratorium also has a popular website, with videos such as one showing the dissection of a cow's eye and answers to questions such as "Why Don't We Have an Eclipse Every Month?"

Pay attention to where information is coming from and remember that fake news more often tends to be outrageous and

Celebrity scientist Bill Nye is a reliable source of information, along with other science experts and sites.

shocking. If a friend does share a story you know isn't true, tell your friend so (kindly). You perform a great service when you bring the truth into the digital landscape today.

Perhaps the best thing to do is to make sure you're getting your "inputs" about the world in many ways—not just via a screen. Talk to friends; talk to family. Have conversations and challenge yourself to explain and prove your opinions when issues come up!

Experience the world by visiting museums, taking books out of the library, attending a science or book talk, joining a book club, or going for a hike and looking at and listening to nature. Put your mobile phone out of reach while you're out exploring the world. Limiting screen time is the best solution. After all, once you're away from the digital world, there are no filter bubbles.

One easy but effective way to fight filter bubbles is to balance screen time with time away from the internet.

ABOUT ELI PARISER

The world knows about filter bubbles thanks to a man named Eli Pariser, who wrote a book and delivered a popular TED Talk about filter bubbles in 2011. (TED Talks are short videos in which thinkers, researchers, scientists, and others talk about ideas or new ways to think about problems and issues.) Pariser's TED Talk has been quite influential—his video has been watched by people more than four million times!

Today, Pariser is head of Upworthy, a company that makes uplifting, informative video stories that are meant to go viral. Upworthy wants the public to pay more attention to critical issues such as sexism, bullying, and racism.

On today's web, thanks in part to "clickbait" headlines and filter bubbles, serious news has been crowded out by junk content: stories, memes, videos designed to shock and even enrage people. Upworthy wants to make it so that people pay attention to serious news and meaningful issues.

That said, Upworthy has used a lot of the techniques associated with clickbait. One common clickbait approach is to frame a video this way: "[A certain thing] happened, and then you won't believe what happens next." Pariser acknowledges that Upworthy was guilty of clickbait headlines. The company has since changed its approach somewhat and toned down the overly dramatic headlines.

GLOSSARY

ad hominem attack In debate, an attack on the person rather than their arguments.

algorithms Mathematical equations used by online companies like Google and Facebook to filter content.

bias Favoring one idea over another; favoring a group of people over another.

clickbait Headlines, titles, and images designed to get people to click on them; often they are misleading.

conspiracy theory A belief based on unproven evidence that some powerful agent such as the government is responsible for events.

critical thinking The ability to consider and analyze problems using reason and argument.

echo chambers Information systems filled with repeated, or continually echoed, ideas and beliefs.

fake news News that is entirely made up, often to benefit a candidate running for office.

filter bubbles A situation that can lead internet users to fall out of touch with diverse experiences and facts because of online filters that feed us personalized content.

flat Earth movement People organized around the belief, despite all evidence to the contrary, that Earth is flat.

internet The global system of connected computers that allows users to browse the web and communicate with people at other connected computers.

media literacy The ability to read the media for hidden factors such as unreliability and personal or political agendas. Someone who is media literate can detect a fake news story and knows how to break out of a filter bubble.

personalization The practice of giving web users content selected specifically for them, made possible by online filters.

social media Online platforms and apps such as Instagram and Facebook through which people connect and share content.

Twitter bot Short for "Twitter robot;" software that pushes out tweets automatically to shape public opinion.

URL Address of a page on the World Wide Web; stands for "Uniform Resource Locator."

World Wide Web System where you can access information online—documents, pages and other content—using a browser such as Chrome. Also known as "the web."

FURTHER INFORMATION

Books

Krieger, Emily. *Real or Fake*? Des Moines, IA: National Geographic Children's Books, 2018.

Paquette, Ammi-Joan, and Laurie Ann Thompson. *Two Truths and a Lie*: *It's Alive!* New York: Walden Pond Press, 2018.

Websites

How Search Works
https://www.google.com/search/howsearchworks

Helpful videos and text from Google demonstrate how the search engine works.

Ways of the Web: Filter Bubbles and the Deep Web: Home
http://guides.library.illinois.edu /c.php?g=348478&p=2347794

This site gives an overview of filter bubbles that is easy to understand and provides tips for "breaking out of the bubble."

Videos

Addressing Hoaxes and Fake News
https://vimeo.com/195753689

In this video, Facebook explains how fake news items are flagged on the site and what to do if you spot a fake news story.

Beware Online "Filter Bubbles"
https://www.ted.com/talks/eli_pariser_beware_online_filter_bubbles

Watch the talk that drew the world's attention to filter bubbles, given in 2011 by Eli Pariser, author of *The Filter Bubble.*

Filter Bubbles and Echo Chambers
https://www.youtube.com/watch?v=Zk1o2BpC79g

View a short video that explains the concepts of filter bubbles and echo chambers and how these affect society.

BIBLIOGRAPHY

Brady, William J., Julian A. Wills, John T. Jost, Joshua A. Tucker, and Jay J. Van Bavel. "Emotion Shapes the Diffusion of Moralized Content in Social Networks." *Proceedings of the National Academy of Sciences* 114(28): 7313-7318. doi:10.1073/pnas.1618923114.

Dewey, Caitlin. "What You Don't Know About Internet Algorithms Is Hurting You. (And You Probably Don't Know Very Much!)" *Washington Post*, March 23, 2015. https://www.washingtonpost.com/news/the-intersect/wp/2015/03/23/what-you-dont-know-about-internet-algorithms-is-hurting-you-and-you-probably-dont-know-very-much/?utm_term=.8682f77bf982.

"Eli Pariser: Beware Online Filter Bubbles." Presented at TED2011, March 2011. TED video, 8:58. https://www.ted.com/talks/eli_pariser_beware_online_filter_bubbles.

Entrepreneur. "Are You Living in a Digital Bubble? This Flowchart Will Tell You. (Infographic)." June 11, 2016. https://www.entrepreneur.com/article/277351.

Google. "How Google Search Works/Overview." 2018. https://www.google.com/search/howsearchworks.

Hanley, Steve. "Researchers Develop Online Game to Inoculate Against Fake News." *Clean Technica*, February 23, 2018. https://cleantechnica. com/2018/02/23/researchers-develop-online-game-inoculate-fake-news.

Jolly, Jihii. "How to Read the News When You're in High School." Medium, February 28, 2016. https://medium. com/future-journalism-project/how-to-read-the-news-when-you-re-in-high-school-8720a60bb2e6.

Kay, Jonathan. *Among the Truthers: A Journey through America's Growing Conspiracist Underground*. New York: Harper, 2011.

Oremus, Will. "Who Controls Your Facebook Feed?" *Slate*, January 3, 2016. http://www.slate.com/articles/ technology/cover_story/2016/01/how_facebook_s_ news_feed_algorithm_works.html.

Pariser, Eli. *The Filter Bubble: What the Internet is Hiding from You*. New York: Viking/Penguin Press, 2011.

"There Are No 'Regular Results' on Google Anymore." DuckDuckGo video. Posted 2013. https://vimeo. com/51181384.

Wall Street Journal. "Blue Feed, Red Feed." Updated hourly. http://graphics.wsj.com/blue-feed-red-feed.

INDEX

ABOUT THE AUTHOR

Jacqueline Conciatore Senter often writes about media and is the author of *Peaceful Protesters: Martin Luther King Jr.* and *The Fourth Estate: The Muckrakers and Progressive Reformers*. She lives in Fairfax, Virginia, with her husband, Michael.